The Indifferent World

Ken Craft

FUTURECYCLE PRESS
www.futurecycle.org

Library of Congress Control Number: 2016931958

Published by FutureCycle Press
Lexington, Kentucky, USA

ISBN 978-1-942371-01-4

For my parents, who set me on the path.
And for Jill, who walks the path with me every day.

Contents

WOODS & LAKE

Trigger.. 11
Barnstorming the Universe.. 12
Halves.. 13
Meditations for November.. 14
Provide, Provide..15
Crows.. 16
School for Earthworms... 17
A Sound Unanswered.. 18
The Sleeping World... 20
3:30... 21
Bug Love.. 22
Sitting in the Dark.. 23
Simplicity..24
Thompson Lake: August 23, 2008...25
Deer Stand...26
Momentary.. 27
A Moth's Digression... 28
June Days After School... 29
Summer's End.. 30
Last Summer Night... 31

HOMEBODIES

Making Gazpacho.. 33
Idyll... 34
Return of the Native...35
Snapper...36
Turgenev Time..37
The F-Bomb Held Hostage.. 38
Keep the Change..39
Waking to Rain... 40
Kitchen Sirens...41
Nested..42
Explorer... 43
Hunting the Unwritten Poem...44
The Recluse..45
Unemployed Cousin.. 46
Freeze Frame..49
The End..50
Homebody...51
Jiggety-Jig..52

MYSTERIES

Another Country.. 55
After the Storm... 56
Triumph of Sisyphus... 57
Epistolary... 58
Tonsillectomy.. 59
Young Brain in a Dairy Barn.. 60
Death Has a Sound.. 61
Cause of Unconsciousness: Great Dane.. 62
Brevity and the Beetle... 63
Somniphobia.. 64
Dog Religion.. 65
Head Cold.. 66
Water Music... 67
Schrödinger's Cat.. 68
Occam's Razor... 69
Falling Stars... 70
Pliny Instructs... 71
Reading Poetry at 4 A.M... 72
Crows & The Reaper... 73
Black Dogs Redux... 74
Mrs. Galway Goes to Night School.. 75

THE INDIFFERENT WORLD

The Death of Narcissus.. 77
Astapova Station.. 78
Dirt Shy.. 79
Jacob Wrestling.. 80
Subterranean.. 81
Universal Truths from the Parlor.. 82
Fire on Scribner Hill... 83
The Physics of Aging... 84
Mortality.. 86
What Is Past... 87
Earthbound.. 88
Samsara.. 89
Insomnia.. 90
The Irony of Lost Cats.. 91
Grave Parable.. 92
Dream of the Yellow Jackets.. 93
Jazz Funeral for Fall... 94

New World Order...95
Song..96
Star Sailor...97
The Builder at Work..98

"The mass of men lead lives of quiet desperation."

—Thoreau, Walden

WOODS & LAKE

Trigger

This is where I held
my breath—
a stand of red pine,
needles and snowdust
scribed about my boot,
cold crescent
resisting a swollen
finger itchy-numb
with November.

This is where a buck
held its breath—
mouth mid-meal
amid the mast,
a single line
of berry drool
spiking the fur
of his white and
wild-cherried chin.

Barnstorming the Universe

The big barn must have landed
overnight, the jolt of its descent
crippling one side so the whole
structure leans south. The white
paint, curly from reentry, looks
foolish as a washed cat.
The roof, too, shows evidence
of atmospheric stress, the mottled
landscape of its green top—tar
paper from missing shingles
probably scattered from Pittsburgh
to Poughkeepsie—having the look
of some moody old bass lurking
in the shallows, scales flaked and
grated at the speed of light.
Incredibly, atop the cupola, a rusted
and outraged weathercock still claws
the ridge. His wattle and comb hang
sideways, one eye searching for
intergalactic beetles, black-backed
fugitives from Andromeda or the
Crab Nebula. A sliding door is ajar,
exhaling the stench of stardust,
of Saturnine ring particulate, of dead
Martians matted on rotted hay.
In the side window, a single shard
of glass clings to the sash. If only
the barn could speak of the yawning
silences, of the teeming nothingness
that peered inside as it hurtled
its way home to this Maine field.

Halves

Shelling the green tongues of pistachios
in September—the steady tick, the fine
nut papyrus riding my lips
before I blow it off — reminds me
of the lake, July, hands scooping, fingers
cracking them open, eating
over wooden salad bowls, kissing,
mouths tender with salt, what
you whispered, the kitchen floor—gray
paint on wide boards—how our soles
held the gloss briefly, sticking.
But the press of shucked bodies
tells a different story, skin smooth,
sheets wrinkled, intersecting lifelines
loath to diverge, to give each other up
to the cool touch of night.

Meditations for November

I.

If raven parabolas
had not seared the sky
above Gibbs Mountain,
it would show no blue
scars, no smoky shearling
gracing its peak.

II.

Is fog
the bottom of a raven's
cry?

III.

As I walk frozen furrows
of corn-stalk carnage,
November's flint
strikes boot soles.
Frost-fire on the field.

IV.

It is warmer
in breathless forest hollows.
The pressed pine needles,
the ghostly essence
of deer.

Provide, Provide

Clem buttresses that old house
with bales of hay against the foundation,
rivets metal roofing over buckled
tar paper, and feeds his splitter, revealing
the striated blond bellies of halved maple
logs and spewing the fine dust of sweet
wood into his khaki-confettied hair.
As if he sat at Job's knee as a child,
that old man stacks his wood into a cord,
builds a square meal for his winter stove,
and doesn't glance up once at the leaden
bottoms of November's indifferent clouds.

Crows

From my cedar-walled study,
I hear them—the scratch
and claw of tar-colored talons
against asphalt—and consider
the tiny avalanches, schist
granules riding the roof's slant.

I've seen them, too,
the caw-bob of heads,
guttural mocks,
challenges, inside jokes.
The way brothers show
love through shove
and insult.

Black Irish, I think,
and what great drinking
buddies my night-glossed
friends would be, the way
they sidle along peaks,
betting on granules, whiling
their raucous lives away.

School for Earthworms

In nature, everything is mouth:
the jaws of a boy's pinch fingers,
the barbed tongue of starved
hooks—their sharp appetites.

Hooks are not sated by silent
twisting and writhing, either.
Worms bleed soil
and blood like some Saint
Segmented Sebastian, but pain
only hardens things; pain whets
cruelty's appetite for martyrs.

One whoosh of breath
and boy casts worm deep
into the wind's esophagus—
paralysis, peristalsis,
the involuntary descent
through air toward the lake's
waiting mouth.

Water: hunger
achy and deep; the surface
speaks, salivates,
swallows. Down line
and lead. The worm
suspends under a white-
hulled bobber, skin
gasping for dirt and stone,
skin crying for air
and earth until slowly,
slowly its impaled life curls
and twists and grows wan
with the waiting—
waiting for a final mouth.

A Sound Unanswered

When you wake early, you make the best of it,
take the dog to the back of the island,
look across the lake to the east shore
where a pine top ignites briefly—
a trick of first light—followed by the quiet dignity
of narrow sunrays sliding between branches.

There's something to be said for a newborn sun,
how cheerful and innocent,
how pregnant with possibility,
nothing like your more forward suns of noon
or your jaded disks of dusk.
Today the sky is streaked with stratus
and the dusky lake shows a watery
black eye, purplish and pink.
Rain, maybe, or humidity lying in ambush
at the noon pass of approaching day.

But now, in stillness as holy as this,
even the dog stops and listens,
his ears arched black tags,
his nose dark pitch trembling
for the scent of chase, the musk of capture.

You hear voices across the water—
fishermen talking each other awake.
And then, downshore, a stick snapping.
The dog's head swivels
and waits on a different silence,
the achy kind swelled by want,
only this time the ache seeps
into clumps of cinnamon fern,
Canada mayflower,
pine needle decay.

All dog disappointment,
he turns his head back, begrudgingly.
Perhaps it's better that the noise
chooses memory over movement
this morning, for I'm of a mood
for the unanswerable
and have no interest
in sudden epiphanies
on an island still asleep.

I take a deep breath while the dog,
nose alive with wet hope,
peers his "Why not's?" at me.

If he only understood: This is why
a man can be married to being alone,
why a man can forget the great "out there"
that is the world; because here,
in the held breath of dawn
on an island gripped by lake,
the world constricts
and, dogs notwithstanding,
men can choose to hear
or not hear, in the case of silences
that punctuate snapped sticks.

The Sleeping World

Stepping the sleeping world
is such splendid isolation.

Walk on the rise of others' breaths,
toe the center soul of hallways,

pry open dark's screen door.
Outside, the kneeling night grows heavy.

It seeps, cracks wild smells
from earth: white-haired roots, grit, stone,

sullen departures. Its ghost gives rise
to pine-top jags and shadows;

the pinking shears-cut sky bleeds
Delft notions of light.

Somewhere in a wood the Horned Owl
8-hoos once, only for you.

It's the fur of loneliness,
those tufts between her talons.

3:30

In the dark
from over the water, a rooster
celebrates my insomnia.

Bug Love

It's hard being a beetle,
mouthing sweet nothings
with mandibles and maxillae.

Still, there's no denying the
sensual of biting and sucking,
of crawling your mate's back

like an amorous-plated
mountaineer ready to fasten his
bolt. Then there's the sixfold

beauty of legs, how they start
in clawing need, end on gripping
seed. If only romance weren't named

Stinkbug, Carrion Bug,
Fungus Bug. If only the hum
and buzz of connubial commerce

and constant hunger
did not attract attention
from puritanical giants.

Sitting in the Dark

In the dark
before dawn,

in the kitchen
before the lake,

when the windows
are rain-runneled

and the room
is still shadow,

I like to sit
and stare at black

glass glaring back,
beady with reflection,

runny with rumination
and the slip of sadness.

Simplicity

When you're broken,
find your Henry David
and simplify. Reach
back, grasp your younger
hand, squeeze and hold
until your palms'
warmth mingles.
Together, walk the woods,
smell distant rain
as it rides westerlies
bareback and brazen.

Forget time. Keep going
through yellow birch and red
maple till you discover
an unmapped pond, sit on
a shoreline boulder,
feel the chill itch
permeate your skin.

Follow the exhaling water
rings when a smallmouth
kisses the surface simply
because it exists, waiting
to be marred with life.

Even fish sense there is
another side, near yet far,
alluring yet fatal,
with many years
to gasp and gulp
at the gilled wonder
of it all.

Thompson Lake: August 23, 2008

Waking to a dog suffering to go out
is no worse than being torn conscious by a phone,
but it isn't pleasant—
and outside, in the snap of dawn,
you miss the warmth of a ceramic mug
cupped in your hands,
the way the tender ghosts of steam
swirl above the coffee,
flirt past your nose,
resolve before your eyes.

Soon, though, as the dog chases a scent ragged
on the back of the island,
you shiver like a dowser stick,
drift toward the lake,
see how it held its breath overnight
until it has turned steely with the waiting.

Now the sun will clear the timber line
and light will bend over eastern shore
where a loon calls from the fog.
The sound takes you back,
reminds you of Wiffle ball tosses with your brother—
the arc and the whistling sound
on these same haunted shores.

Still water at dawn
has a way of doing that,
putting you on the trail of a separate scent:
the whiff of the past.
There's the loon, of course,
the drawn-out cry of regret,
and the nuthatch circling the pine tree,
its feet scratching against bark
like a gnawing conscience.

Out on the dock, the Adirondack's flat arm
holds last night's glass,
melted ice,
drowned gnats.
Then the cold nose against the back of your hand,
the wagging tail of a newly born day
just as the sun clears the point,
just as the water softens to silver,
and, like a seeing-eye guide,
the dog leads you back into the camp.

Deer Stand

Here I hold a soft silver something
in the rapidly draining dark, my thermos
weakly phosphorescent in the slow-breaking
November dawn. Like the Buddha of Frostbite,
I sit twenty feet above forest undergrowth
eyeing a deer path crossed only by dead
leaves and old scat. Down-to-earth, it climbs
a hill even with my view, mocking
such stratagems as wooden stands
creaking between the crotches of oak
and maple. So pour hour-old camp coffee,
inhale its ghostly tendrils, invoke
the absent-minded god of hearth and home,
imagine black-iron omelets and sourdough
toasts, buttered suns setting into scratchy centers.
At my side, colder fare—camera, Moleskine,
chewed Ticonderoga, and that Chekhovian
prop, the rifle. I mention this because it
does not go off by the end of the poem, not
while bedding bucks and does, compressed pine
needles under blood-warm bellies in the fur-white
wind, watch me shiver from an indifferent distance.

Momentary

Drone of an outboard;
then, out of the cove, trout-scale
glint of an aluminum boat
unzipping the water.
On its back bench,
a teenaged boy, eyes squinting
into future's glare, hair
and unbuttoned shirt flapping
the past. I thought it odd,
so early, while his kind slept,
but he was not so much boy
as all boys and none of them.
In fact, once, caught by a sun
cut and pried from new sky,
he was me—the *was* in me.

I wanted to wave because,
in that expiring moment, he existed;
he could not wave because, hidden
by tree-shadowed pine and pitch,
I could not exist. I knew I'd never see
it again: how his grip squeezed
the throttle's shake, how his arm
and elbow notched an angle
from the airy plane between back
and forward motor.

Such vision could only emerge
over water, be spied
from a sure-footed shore of sin,
with a Mercury's
20-horse hum dimming
and dying like gnats
whose glory is only moment.

Boat, boy—both disappeared,
arcs crowning Hayes Point:
geometry of transience,
intersection of time, creators
of a dark and widening wake,
half coming for me.

A Moth's Digression

It was only a lunate zale moth, that hole
on my study wall.

I placed my hand over it, then slowly
slid it shut

until the cupped darkness fluttered
and my deaf palm

felt a whispering inside. Outside,
slowly opening its cell,

I saw the moth's mantle of fur, the soft
chips of dust its wings brushed

on the Zen garden groove of fingertips.
A nudge and it flew, ascending

until a barn swallow hit it mid-flight,
leaving a brief hole in the air.

June Days After School

In late June
the days yawn
and sleep
like dusty hounds.
Mornings, limber
and lazy as
Huck Finn rafting
under shifting pipe
smoke, induce
their pleasant dirge
of distance: the lawn mower,
the chainsaw and cicada song.

Slowly
the current of time carries the days.
They spin downstream
in dreamy swirls and eddies,
leagues away toward the closing shores,
toward the rising roots of July.

At night, remains
of afternoon haze
drift skyward. They etch
a shadow river, plow
the heavenly fabric with
with a milky blade, ever flowing
south where an estuary of stars
snag on sandbars of
possibility.

Summer's End

In the dog days, when Altair and Deneb
set toward western waters, Vega
flaring in their starry wake, the choir
of peepers and crickets melds liquid
to languid; the first maple leaves ripen
and curl to red fists; pine needles spread
gold scripture across the water;
nuthatch feet circle tree trunks—
gentle scriveners
scribing the dawn of dying days.

Last Summer Night

At night, out on the float,
planks cool against bare
feet and back, still lake still
speaking in slurps
between barrels beneath,
I listen from this distant
outpost to the tender whine
of tires on 26, a restless
language I shouldn't know.
Above, cheeping brown bats flutter in
insect-dizzy circles and, before long,
my eyes adjust and the sky
ripens and cracks down the middle,
revealing a powdery streak
glinting with shards from an ancient
anvil. I am the last man
on earth to lift my finger, trace
the vector of Altair, Deneb, and Vega
against the vault of
the smithy's floor.
And the tires on 26 whine.
And the fish over dark
marl and eelgrass wait.

HOMEBODIES

Making Gazpacho

August, sun setting on the lee
side of the beach house, nothing
but you, me, the heat, avocados
and chips.

I find a food
processor and peel the fruits
with a paring knife. You say, "Let
me clean them," take each pit in your
mouth, roll it softly,
thoughtfully as your cheeks belly
side to side.

I stop to watch
as you spit them into your palm,
birthing three pits, laying
them like Zen meditation
balls on the cutting
board.

"Good Christ," I say.
"I'm hungry," you reply.

Frozen peas in the tin cup
cling to the curved
insides. I finger them out.

Lemon juice, salt, pepper. Pump
of the processor. Then, just before we
share, olive oil
in promiscuous swirls and loops,
a stream of gold garland
celebrating the soup's surface.

I take out the white ceramic
bowls. You smile, stray green flesh
at the corner of your mouth
like a soft shoot of summer grass.

Idyll

Each day brings the wedding closer:
clapboard and trim painters,
window washers, florists, a house
under siege.

I wish
I were a Bruegel peasant
far away, under a sky pricked and paled
by August sun:

Scythes whistle. Sweat-soaked muslin
kisses our backs. Kerchiefed
maidens swing in rhythm, while a rick
wagon with wheat-strained ribs
waits in back, swaddling its shade,
its cool, corked jugs.

Let us stop here
and rest, limbs splayed
with the sweetness
of fatigue. Let us drink this wine.
Open these wicker baskets.
Find the airy white hearts
of crust-cased loaves with our thumbs.

Return of the Native

In the beach house you don't own you walk barefoot
over knotted slats of wood, soles scrimmed gray

with dust. The door, left ajar by yesterday's heat,
has let the lonely sounds of a conch inside.

It hides somewhere and nowhere, inner walls
scoured smooth and hard from its narrow breath.

In the beach house you don't own the widow walks
her sentence, squinting over the heaving syntax.

On the second floor lies the captain's library—the only
literate room—a bookshelf, a bone of knuckle coral,

a piece of driftwood light as time. The barometer
is bottom-broken; the bubbling tidal flats give up

their dead; the seagulls tilt over the rot
of eyeless dogfish. The code of hospitality stands

outside the beach house you don't own. Its heels
sink in the wet give, hair slow-dances the wind.

Someone who doesn't live here is in the kitchen
baking jonny cake in iron skillets. Someone

who doesn't read here has left the book open,
red silk marker bleeding at the crease.

Someone who didn't die here is sailing home
wearing salt and sweat, wool and regret.

Snapper

Atop the ridge near the driveway,
small ramparts of sandy
dirt behind her, a snapping
turtle lays her eggs
at dusk. Her eyes,
heavy-lidded, blink with boredom
at her audience. Supreme
in her ill-chosen spot,
her helmet of stink,
the algae like wet war ribbons
clinging to her carapace,
she appears exhausted
with ancientness. Behind
lies the dark tale
of her reptilian conscience;
in front, the set jaw
of resignation, resolve.
"It'll be gone tomorrow," I tell
my son. "All of it."
The next morning, in place
of the snapper, a hole well
dug and white leather
casings—hollow
remnants of raccoon
rapture—and somewhere,
down in the bog, mud
and indifference.

Turgenev Time

As a young man, I lay in a finished
basement for years, bound
to an oatmeal carpet, sickly and citrus-skinned
in the tangerine glow of incandescent bulbs.
Outside it was winter in Connecticut; far
away it was Hell in Vietnam; but inside it was merely
hard Berber rug, a gas heater,
and my gentrified Russian novels.
The knot-paneled room offered neither hope
nor despair nor thought of escape. Warm-woozy,
I dozed, awakened, read
more as the heater exhaled
comfort.

In the books, lime trees rattled and rooks took wing.
Bough to fragrant leaf, kvas-drinking peasants
laughed and cursed. On the wind came the smells
of horse and rain and superfluous ideas.
Outside it was spring in Oryol; inside it was
black-backed Penguins, ocher-edged paper,
ink in Monotype Bembo, the chalky outline
of my sun-starved body on the floor.

I remember my mother's art deco clock, gold spikes
gripping the dark pine wall, how it dripped
hours and minutes, weighing tick for heavy tick
with the pinging heater, submerging
me and my future pasts—all of them—
in the calm killing current of Turgenev time.

The F-Bomb Held Hostage

Four-letter words, healthy as mongrels,
climb etymological trees like monkeys

at home on any branch,
hanging from any appendage, indulging

in any seen or obscene pastime.
King of the Troop is the GI Joe

of 4-letter words, the F-Bomb.
In a fit of *faux wisdom,*

my grandfather once taught
that you could judge a man's intelligence

by the number of f-bombs he leavened
his speech with—the more you hear,

the dumber the speaker. I often wonder
how he would have reacted if I replied,

"Fuck that." But no. I only thought it. For
I have yet to forge a separate peace

with the f-bomb, fearing it like
Alzheimer's, convinced if I let fly

like the movies or soldiers on leave,
all that I have learned will begin to leak

from my brain like flatulent helium
from some politely sagging balloon.

Keep the Change

I hate change,
how the clink
in the pockets
reminds me
of Magwitch
on the moors,
of unpennied
penury, of Dickens'
debtor prisons
and Dodo-like
five-and-dimes.

Give me the
quiet of paper
currency, greasy,
green, suspiciously
hungover
like U.S. Grant,
for I love the feel
of folded wads,
of crumpled cash—
soft, legal, and
tender in any state
I find myself.

Waking to Rain

Waking to rain
is a lovely sadness
for ears to sip
under sheets of darkness.

Fat pats keep a muffled beat
in shingle-crazed beads; watery
timpani drone meditations
through guttural tunnels.

Downstairs, the dog whimpers.
Push back the spell, pull feet
from their cottony folds
and rills, and thud down the flights.

After, he'll drag his wet
wolf smell into the house,
musk tethered tight. After,
his fur-spiked shake

will measle the wall
by the door, blessing it
like holy water cast by bishops
from the archdiocese of rain.

Kitchen Sirens

Drinking people are loud people. This is lost
on children, who make monkey bars of noise,
climbing through and over its steel pipes
until they king the metal smell of mountain.
I should know. As a boy I sat atop that world
down a long hall I no longer walk.
The kitchen sounds, though: the hollow
clink of ice cubes sharpening tall glasses,
the pour-gurgle of cheap whiskey, vodka,
Bacardi rum—hell, even gin was welcome then—
the laughter and competing voices: Mom's, Dad's,
uncles' and aunts' and cousins' like cloudy
fruit flies circling life's sweet deadlies.
They well up lazy with the fermentation
of time, attenuated but holding
the fraught rope of years.
And here, up the lengthening
passage, far from 60s kitchens stocked
for drinking as much as cooking,
the friendly smell of cigarette smoke
still sniffs me out.
Like a museum at night, lights dimmed,
the closed display never changes.
It's still Saturday night. It's still Bicycle cards
and coins, potato chips and onion dip, fondue
and the Sterno's eternal flame.
Sometimes, stupidly, I grow jealous
of the happily dead down that hall.
Like Odysseus strapped to nostalgia's killing mast,
I listen longer than I should.

Nested

There is a knack
to flying, yes,
but why would a fledgling,
blanketed in feathered
grass, bowered by leafs
swaying humid-green
in spring winds?
Here cricket leg, ivory grub,
and bloodied worm drop
from a saffron-beaked sky.
Here night falls languid
and the moon tears loose
from heaven's starry thicket,
softly breaking, softly setting,
burnishing the pewter branches
as it passes in gentle delight.

Explorer

My older brother hung
upside down from the top bunk,
his hair a precocious beard, his
eyebrows smiling *u*'s beneath
low-lidded eyes, his nose-trunk
fluted in freckled
majesty, canopied by nostrils
sniffing at a tooth-and-tongue
hole-punched like a Cyclops'
eye in his forehead.

Eventually his head swelled
with gravity and he crept crooked
from the room. I climbed to con
his big-brother secrets, falling back
down under, gripping the side guard
with backs of my knees,
stretched in dangle-armed glory.

I discovered a hidden room
with doors you step over
to exit. Their frames
reached a ceiling where
carpet kissed straight
lips of hardwood, where one slip
dropped you into the quick-slurry
of swallowing floors, where poisonous
mushroom bulbs waited
to explode and electrocute
intruders.

Even so, I wanted to drop
into this puree of white,
to get swallowed for good, to go
the manly way of all explorers
remembered as unsolved
mysteries, burial
site unknown.

Hunting the Unwritten Poem

You see them in the mercury
light of water, the expanding
orbs of silver where trout
breathe. You hear
them in the sleepy kiss
of rainfall on pine
needles, smell them
as if they were snow
to the west.

Like a dead bird's eye,
they lose luster
the moment you kill them
to glean their mysteries. They
close mute membranes,
hide. From across the field,

a crow's dark instincts
distinguish men with sticks
from men with .22s.
Poems are world-wary, too. Hear
the whistle of wing lift
as they take flight.

The Muse keeps time
with Dali's clocks of melt.
Look again—an
unwritten poem shifting
in the wind, an open
wound of torn air.

The Recluse

You might catch her outside, hurrying, burdened
by the shell of hair and flesh. Sometimes her head cocks left
in robin-thought, hearing the sounds
of her fathers tunneling through the centuries:
wind combing pine trees; branch-to-branch limb scrapes;
sweet chickadee cheeps.

But she hears things her fathers never did, too: the harsh
gargle of Harleys, the distant down-gearing of diesel
engines, the sky-slicing jet-blare of white.
Somewhere there's a chainsaw chewing
trees till they're blond and weepy. Somewhere there's
a highway humming the rubber-treads of lonely,
like a sound trying to starve
and fade, wheels force-fed the sadness.

Suddenly she flinches. Through the door, toward
the nest, into the cool of cross and beam, tongue
and groove, stainless steel nail and
aluminum ductwork. Cosseted by drywall.
Softened by moss paint. Refuge.

Inside the insides, constricting within her constrictions,
smaller shells still: Bedding for the soul.
Sepia pictures mouthing "mother" in an olive
tongue. Shades shut and sleepy. Clock-ticks eternal.
Shells curling on themselves: the napping cat,
dozing dog, self-spun nautilus.

Here, deep within days in the dark
by a dim square light, she writes.
Language for language's sake—meaning her
meanings, which, if she returns to weeks
later, she forgets, frightened, as if a stranger
broke into the fortress and left a suicide note.

Unemployed Cousin

I.

For a guy living alone,
his kitchen looks
perpetually partied down.
The Formica countertop, a fading blue
sea, pocked with cracker-
crumb islands and the half-moon
stains of can-bottom atolls.
A Krakatoa of dishes,
forks and spoons, dried hamburger,
Ragú sauce, and beer cans
rises from the sink.
He scratches 5-day growth
on his neck. He says,
"This place depresses me."

II.

"Remember Misquamicut
when we were kids?" he asks.
He begs me to drive him,
to shell him from the hardening
walls of this apartment,
the Internet sites he can't stop
checking, the 55″ television screen
glowing yellow and blue
like JFK's eternal flame.
"Christ, how do you afford
all this," I ask.
His eyes swell like a goldfish's.
"Think I am," he says,
"a fucking savage?"

III.

At first, crystals of morning sun
playing the windshield, open passenger
window whipping his hair,
he talks about the bridge over the creek,
the smell of salt and seaweed
and teenage bravura,
how we jumped, how the cold
water forced us up like corks.
"Remember lying on the beach all day,"

he asks, "the chicks checking my body
out?" I look at his body. All this time
off, and he apparently hasn't.
He means a body caught
in the amber of time, the one
under Joe Weider dumbbells
on a cracked-vinyl bench.
"Yeah, those were good times,"
he says. "That time with the chick
from Jersey underwater? Taking
her with a thousand clueless
people right there on the beach?"
(It's one of those things—a passenger
who's forgotten the car
includes a driver.)

IV.

July traffic on 1A. Nostalgia thickens
like syrup, crusts, hardens,
stops like it's just another Ford
braking in the sludge of traffic. "Take
the damned breakdown lane
why don't you," he says,
tapping time on the glove compartment,
constantly changing radio stations.
At the beach, he swears at sand
burning the frog-belly whites
of his soles. No chicks
from Jersey admire the middle-aged
dough of his stomach. The waves,
smaller than memory's, heave
with jellyfish. "What the hell
happened here?" he wonders aloud.

V.

Not even out of Westerly, he's asking
about packies. "Let's pull over, get
some Pabst and a few nips
for the trip back."
"Let's?" I say. "Staties might have
something to say about that."
"OK, me. I'll pay you back.
You know, when I get a job."
He glances out his window

then, the passenger-side mirror
reflecting words like lemons
in his mouth.
I swore I wouldn't anymore,
but who the hell am I?
Ahead lies blue Formica,
the sink, its volcanic bile
marking the days.
I pull off. I give him a twenty.
I listen to the jingle
of bells as he passes
through the door.

Freeze Frame

Our shoes pin long shadows to dead
grass. We lean like Easter morning
happened not to our yard but to the deck

of a Cunard liner in heavy seas. Gram
has the damned fox stole curling
her gingerbread neck. In her left hand,

Mom has a clutch by the throat, in her
right, Billy's bunched collar. Her grim
smile speaks to the rictus of her grip.

A shadow lies prostrate before
us, head fedora-forged, arms raised
in supplication. Forgive us, father.

The End

I am boxing books, revealing the clean canvas
of each bookshelf's back. It looks like a wall
of blank pages now—smooth, squared caves

gleaming. White niter squinting against the light
of day. Like shelling oysters, I pry classics
and forgotten bestsellers away and the bookshelf

bares its opal throat to the glaring world.
How quickly I undo years of reading. How
swiftly the hallowed becomes hollowed.

Some books slip neatly into their cardboard
coffins: the moderns who mimicked the greats,
the greats who lingered too long

like shelf squatters. Now Virginia Woolf
and Mrs. Dalloway sip tea in an unlit
lighthouse; William Faulkner lies dying;

and, in a certain slant of sunlight, F. Scott
Fitzgerald looks both beautiful and damned.
All crowded in a boxed row of dust

and spine and spite. Twice, at the last moment,
I hear the muffled voice of inscriptions—
a college roommate replacing my lost

Catcher in the Rye with this oxblood
paperback. My wife, a young girlfriend
again, whispering, "Nothing gold can stay"

on the yellowing page of collected
Frost. And so I decide quickly as I go,
sensing, as the executioner does, that speed

silences a pining conscience. I know
I'm done when I find a stiff dollar-bill
bookmark halfway through Joyce's *Ulysses*.

It marks the end of a reading voyage and—for
some Penelope or Telemachus on a library lawn—
a new start arrived from this distant shore.

Homebody

The house? The order of your architect,
then? What of the rain, its gentle
riverbedding on your window, the teardrop's
slow shimmy like someone else's pain
staring in? And outside, the sun after
warming earth and tar until they surrender
their spectrals—ribbons for the heavens.

The house is a neatly creased gift,
yes—its empty, heated squares,
its predictable mazes, cagey
balusters, muntins, and mullions.
But leaving a house is emancipation,
too, a walk from the prison bars of self—
the ones you've gripped your whole life,
so cool, so smooth.

Jiggety-Jig

They say you can't go home again,
so I did.

Two decades' drought made my childhood
home hard as a sponge dried of memory.

When I was eight, Grandpa
gave me that anatomy book and said,
"Boy, don't ever get in the habit
of seeing people as smiling skeletons
just because you know what's under the lid."
But teeth were just bones after that
and eyes just sockets to the soul.

So with the house. Mere skeletal
parts now: concrete dandruff
under front-step risers, squinting
windows, a show of moss stubble
on the shingles.

There's the rusting oil pipe near the back
wall, at least, calling
"wait a minute" real friendly-like.
"Don't ever let me see you sniffing
that again," Mama once warned.
And I didn't. Till now.
No cars in the driveway, so what
the hell. I steal over, twist the metal cap,
deep-toke 80-proof vapors of heating oil.
Sweet Jesus, I think, taking more drags.
Real as a rib!

The corner garden?
A garden of gone now.
All those hours and days as a juvenile
inmate pulling weeds by the hair,
shaking dirt from the legs.

I give the back door
the look—the one reserved
for folks who cultivate dandelion,
chicory, and clover from fake
leather La-Z-Boys.

"Can I help you with something, sir?"

Jesus, but I jump. A man. Framed
by my old bedroom window yet.
I'm disoriented. Heating-oil haze,
maybe. Looks like Dad blurried by screen
storm. Or Father Kelly's shadow-whispers
at the dark grille of the confessional
in Sacred Heart.

"I used to live in this house," I smile
with all the confidence of the condemned.

"That's nice," he says. "But maybe you should
be going now instead of standing
in other people's back yards."

Other people. So *they're* the ones. Saying
you can't go home again, I mean.

I hate being kicked in the ass
by a platitude.

MYSTERIES

Another Country

Under the frozen dome of December
mornings, the scrim of dawn
not even an orange thread
caught in the eastern branches,
I often marvel at the dog's earthly
preoccupations when my nose,
called to greater heights, sniffs
at the cold and dry scent of the heavens.

His cold black snout, quivering
over a stale snowbank claimed
yesterday by some stray adversary,
is oblivious as the alpha dog
above us herds stars
and bounds at the heels
of his boreal master, belted
and deliberate in his stride.
In my heart I know that the crunch

of my blind boots in this darkness
carries an unearthly echo, that the stride
of the hunter heading for a hearth
deep under the western horizon
crackles over another country,
its frozen furrows black and uneven,
its broadcast ice studding the endless way.

After the Storm

Wind fans the puddles
on the walk and the dark fabric
of clouds has torn
apart, bleeding blue
and white coagulate, spraying
the earth with light.

Why do I look to the shifting
sky and think of time
punctures? Why am I sure
the airy hollows
lead to a hidden self—
younger, healthier,

ignorant with muscle
and grace? That me
is no acolyte to answers.
This me sees pools
of repeating selves and steps
through them.

Triumph of Sisyphus

Sunlight as skewering
spit. I slap Sisyphus
on his sweaty back,

say, "Damn, another
day. Time conspires
against us,

but we've taken
the rock and made
a flint of our hatred."

Then I press hands
and head against
the igneous injustice

of it all, pushing,
heeding the harsh
sound of stone-

scraped mountain.
I am ashamed
of the resentment

I secret from him,
from his metallic
stench. I am wary

of the sparks of mica
and silence in his
hair, the dark

delta of
soot and salt
and subordination

glinting in slow
tributaries
across his ribcage.

Side by side, the lie
of my muscle, bone,
coddled resentment,

and his grunts
close as the starved
air ruling a well.

Epistolary

It's Sunday and my head aches.
I wrap cup after cup
of coffee around it, swaddling
these morning temples,
compressing that small pulsing
vein on the left—the one
your finger traced as a tributary
of the Lethe whose silt, you said,
empties into the Hades of my head.

But you asked about the weather
outside, not inside.

Yesterday's rain—raw
as the cold trout you held
at the lake, the heft of his belly
like a silver "u" between
your hands (you called
it "gratifyingly bourgeois")—
has been broomed out
to sea: the Gulf of Maine, the Bay
of Fundy, straight up the Vikings'
hairy nostrils, for all I care.

Inside after outside is always cozier
than inside without the contrast.
It's a metaphor like everything
else. A stubborn metaphor,
maybe. Like us. Or the shifting
clouds that swap names
outside our windows each day.

Cumulus. Cirrus. Stratus. Alto-this.
Nimbus-that. Go on.
Get out of bed. Check your sky
and think of me waiting
down here. Then write what you see
and send it sooner. So your questions
match the season, at least.
Please?

Tonsillectomy

At nine I watched the big-animal
veterinarian help a farmer
and his son wrestle a horse
to the ground, binding his feet
into a flinty bouquet of hooves.
Once he hit dirt, that horse
fought like Vermont's indifferent
earth might break open
and swallow him hide and mane,
but it was useless with his feet
bunched like tight crabapples
and the men pressing down
above the petrified milk of his
eyes. When the knife flashed
like sun-struck whitewater,
I asked what he was about.
The vet, unshaven, smelling
of armpit and Red Man, took
my little frame in and paused.
"Taking his tonsils out, son,"
he said. Then, when the rich
red line bloomed under the knife,
spreading between the horse's
back legs, the beast shuddered
and gasped an unhorselike cry.
Turning away, I clutched myself,
for although many of my friends'
had, my tonsils had yet to come out.

Young Brain in a Dairy Barn

At the fault line of my brain,
toeing the tectonic plates
of memory: that vet, that farmer,
and that cow, its calf nearby but separated.
"I'm going for the afterbirth," the vet
explained. "Sometimes, after a calf is born,
the placenta stays behind
and that's not good
for the mother, understand?"
I nodded. Just another manure
morning in Vermont, me a 9-year-old
in the cool marrow of bone-colored barn.
I inhaled the smell of iodine, hydrogen
peroxide, and rubber as the vet rolled
a python-sized glove past his elbow.
His arm dull as brown laundry
soap, his fingers doing a few calisthenics,
he squirted a solution along his
bound hand and arm, lifted the cow's tail,
and eased his hand inside the fleshy
hole. The cow and I, equally surprised,
jumped together. Then the vet set
his boots, his legs a wishbone
of dried mud. A puff of air broke his lips
as he pushed and the cow rocked
and the head-gate rattled. It was like the cow's
puckered mouth had migrated back, bit down
on a man's arm, swallowing
it in steady sips. The vet was up to his
shoulder, his eyes on a high, dimly lit
window gauzed in spider webs.
He seemed to think with his hidden
hand; his eyes moved as if interpreting a foreign
tongue. When the eruption came, his arm
shot out before a shower of cow turd
splattering the floor. "Shit!" he shouted,
as if 9 years made me some damned fool.
The farmer, wearing buffalo plaid shirt,
suspenders and, until that moment,
no expression, grinned. "Friend or enema?"
he drawled. "Enemy," I corrected. With
more than a little pride, too.

Death Has a Sound

It was great living forever
but now it's over
and for the first time
I hear silence—until noises
crowd it out:
an approaching hearse; rainwater
peeling the arc of wheel wells;
the engine of a plane
building in timbre, fading, dying,
its contrail the line of a chair leg scraping
the long, clouded floor.

Lonely sounds. And there's nothing
lonelier than thinking you're
a breech-birth punching your Lazarus dome
through death's airy membrane, blood
reincarnate, shards of stars
reconstellating in your hair.

Just like that, with its famous poise,
death postpones. I know
when I hear the pipework
of a rebellious stomach—work ethic
primeval, *apologia* of
a body bent on immortalities.
And then, the familiars: clock
ticking, heat register pinging,
clink of the jailer's keys.

Cause of Unconsciousness: Great Dane

the police report read after Jean-Jacques Rousseau
took his solitary walk in search of reverie
but was flipped by a dog charging into twilight.
The great philosopher awoke to the Braille
of cool gravel under his back, looked
through a sieve of linden leaves, saw the sifting stars
and traced constellations against the crystallizing sky.
For one slippery moment, he enjoyed no recall
of past or future, victory or defeat, Voltaire or Madame d'Ormoy.
Instead he was stricken by a lonesome present
where he floated in the lazy pools of new eyes,
inhaling earth and stars like a child, sensing soft spasms
of a life he had not lived and would quickly lose
if he dared stand up and brush off enlightenment.

Brevity and the Beetle

In the garage I saw a black beetle,
a lumbering sunflower seed
plodding the cold floor.
I chose an empty
yogurt cup
and scooped him up.

Cupped and docile, he rode
the crease into my study, where I found
the *Field Guide to North American Spiders & Insects.*
The deal, I assured him, was freedom
if he wasn't born for blood or bark.

He was unmoved by threats,
as if time were his mate,
and endured patiently,
oval and dark,
an ivory half moon
about his armored shoulders.
If only he wore his antennae lower,
the mustache would cast him as villain.
But this was me;
he was built for modesty.

He never once scritched the sides
of his solitary as if to mime escape.
And if wings were in his arsenal,
he felt no need to advertise.

Photo found on 550, he was exposed
as an American carrion beetle—agent
of the already dead and subject
of guidebook poetry:
"Locates carrion by scent, alights,
and crawls quickly out of sight."

Outside, I set him free and he withdrew,
an unhurried undertaker
off to reclaim the Earth's own,
reseeding her womb, bedding her dead,
easing us into eternity.

Somniphobia

She says it's always been the way, how she embraces sleep
like some sweet narcotic.
As cold crawls up the sheets
between us, she quips, "Sleep—it's the new sex,"
and I wonder which daytime show she heard it on
instead of laughing like I'm supposed to
and would have when I was fun.

Then comes the mockery of her breathing—so soon,
so deep, I think pretend.
I'm left alone—me and consciousness again.
Clock sounds
ferment in the dark.
Second-ticks wall in the silence,
tongue and groove.
They sow brain fissures,
percussion's pale sprouts pushing into the ear
till I lift head from pillow
only to sense them again, dislodged from arterial net,
beating the bars of my ribcage,
bottom-feeding on bone.

I wish the dark gone. I wish to surprise
dawn stealing inside this room, quiet and lovely,
like sand threading the night's hourglass,
like her hand when it cupped
the curve of my shoulder and squeezed
warmth into my fear.

Dog Religion

Each morning he rises and bows
before me—parable of humility,
maw yawning, paws splaying.

The hollow rattle of dry meal
raining on his aluminum bowl
pops his ears. Every day,
novelty in the ritual of repetition;
every day, the Pavlovian ear perk.
Like heartbeats and bad breath,
autonomous tail and tongue.
Just so.

Waiting for me
to move, he approaches the orb
demurely, noses in, crunches the bland
and the brown. That lovable greed.
Those stained, pacifist teeth.

He feeds, license and rabies tag
keeping time at bowl's edge. And always,
in the end, one dry kibble
is left in a bowl cirrus-streaked
with spit: his offering
to the food gods, his prayer
answered each miraculous day.

Head Cold

The head stands amazed,
harboring labyrinths of lead,

Minotaur of mucus
struggling to ford rivers

that forgot their flow.
Mythical horns scratch

glyphs across the sinal
Lascaux, itching,

yearning for escape
through impassable passages:

eyes branched in red
lightning, nose non-negotiable,

mouth agog and dug dry
with rhythmic rushes of air.

Water Music

Sounds fish make in their aquariums
are like the lazy whir of ceiling fans
churning soft lacunas on humid
Florida nights. In the more perfectly
pellucid orbs of goldfish, it's the fat-
lipped do-wop, the cupped trumpet,
mouths keeping quarter time. The lake
trout's silver-spotted song slides
in marly modulation beneath the eel's
long note, the large-mouth's deep bass.

For cacophony, consider the ocean
at high tide, its wind-scalloped dome
reverberating with acoustics
of rising scales below. A mute music
box, the nautilus circles round the sound
of its own secret, the unheard dirge of
drowned chords. For counterpoint,
in shadowy orchestral pits, muffled
evensong of sailors, ribs like pale reeds
chanting largo in depth's dulcet dusk.

Schrödinger's Cat

I think on that small specimen
of captured night, the cat
it contains, how conundrum's
wet nose sniffs along the seam

of walls and paradox, whiskers
twitching with the itch
of *reductio ad absurdum.*
Maybe the skeleton steps lively

inside its fine fur, probing
the hide that scientists must
ponder from another side; maybe
the body shows muscular

curiosity about its world,
keeping the faith in daylight,
holding to the creed and salvation
of the finite number 9.

Occam's Razor

Before leaving the room, cognitive
scientists asked him, "How many
uses for this razor can you think

of? You have two minutes, 38 seconds.
Go." And, sweat poxing his taxed brow,
he wanted to add, "...to Hell," but no,

he needed this job, so he considered
that flat, rectangular world against
the polished mahogany table, the *terra*

firma of rust mapping its side.
"Well, you could scrape rogue paint
flecks off a window," he said

seemingly to himself, though he
assumed he was being observed
through some painting or plastic

plant or thermostat by the goat-beards
with their white coats and clipboards.
"Or start a collection of razor-thin

margins, or make cutting remarks
at cocktail parties or even business
meetings, or drop it down the slit

inside a medicine cabinet and wonder,
or loan it to a suicide for wristwork
or a blood bank for withdrawals,

or begin a rust-removal experiment
employing any number of letters
from the Table of Elements."

The door burst open, slamming
the wall. "Absolutely not! Entirely
wrong! Possibly insane! Simply

stated, this razor is designed to
shave cheekiness like yours—hair
off the chin and neck. Now then,

the next question. If you were a razor,
what kind of razor would you be? You
have one minute, 13.6 seconds. Go...."

Falling Stars

I am cow-eyed staring at sky
before dawn, anchored by this leashed lab.

He tracks cottontail
contrails through the grass's frost

as my headlamp mines the stars
for falling facets, brief lines of interrogation.

My head, white alpha
star of the constellation spinal, bends back,

exhales, launching lit ghosts,
haunted smoke rings to wed the moon.

Pliny Instructs

(after Annie Dillard's *Pilgrim at Tinker Creek*)

Though he did not bear witness himself, Pliny
shared stories of Portuguese mares that raised
flapping tails to the gale so they would
conceive foals swift as the wind.
Pity the Portuguese stallions, ears bent back
in stiff Iberian blasts, enduring heirs
apparent from southerlies off the sea!
What Pliny left out in his provincial Roman fancy
were the lady sockeyes of Alaska,
how they turned tail to the river, pectoral fins
fanned against the rush, heads blunted
against bracing flow, rocking to the slippery
lust of arched air over whitewater ecstasy.

Reading Poetry at 4 A.M.

Poetry is best read
in the thin hours,
when words and light
explore as if for the first time,
when eyes scan the bright and shadow
of syntax, walk the diction primeval,
find font's canyons on day's
struck page.

It's mornings when lines break
under the rhythm of crow call,
their gentle rocking of sky, black and forth,
black and forth.

A line, too, can be lifted by a cardinal's
match-head strike of pine
when it sings the lonely,
the reddest tassel in the wood.

Lines can be herded by the green memory
of hemlocked stanzas too; sometimes
they are scraped smooth by a cricket's
night legs still hot with song.

That a poem prefers readings
from dawn's breviary
is a metaphor halved, its soft flesh
opened and musky, redolent
of a certain ripeness searching the koan
of its other half, enjambment
still hard on the vine.

While others sleep, you can listen
for a poem's metered pulse. You can breathe,
smell its incense, but only
in the nave of morning.

Crows & The Reaper

In life they fly profligate, shreds of black bunting
tossed in updrafts. They celebrate
the sky's long memory, announce each other,
call down the clouds, laugh, mock;
they are sidling fops in November fields,
hell-raisers among razed cornstalks;
they are the black pupils of God glaring down
from buzzing overhead wires, from the leafy lifelines
of oaks, from the hollow well of the sun's ear.
In death? No one knows, but never a tangle
of talon, tail, and char on the street, wing feather
waving in each car's wake. Instead, absence
of evidence and death assumed—just as
the shadow behind mostly moves as you do.

Black Dogs Redux

The blue sad light is on again.
Maybe it's the weather. Or the season.
Or the relentless grind of the quotidian.
Maybe it's the "Is that all there is?" of the holidays,
where boxing ornaments, burning dried holly, and recycling
wrapping paper feels like picking up
after the dogs. The black dogs. Who heel all too well.
Orion has his astral-eyed pooch;
I have my black-furred dogs, loyal as shadow.

Walking backwards, man's best friend is god, who has a hand
in this. That's the sensation: the Great One's hand applies
a slight pressure to my head, weighing me down.
The motivation to read? Nothing seems good anymore.
To write? I have nothing to say
and, damn *Ecclesiastes* anyway, it's all been said.
Everything is vanity, all right, a striving after wind.
And like the Greek chorus, there's this 33-degree rain
at 5 in the morning. Not the silent, deflected sound of snow
but that direct, cold ping running down the gutters of my spirit.

I adjust the sad light so the angle is better,
file rays in the blue facets of my eyes,
reshuffle them, come up with a deeper blue: slow, indigo
in scope. I can always sleep, but sleep leaves ash dreams.
I know exercise is an antidote, but I must first scale
the architecture of my own apathy. All those slivers under the fingernails!
It's easier to eat ice cream that never judges.
Scoop of here in a cone of now.

Didn't Ben Franklin say we should be well-rounded, after all?
He said a lot. And never once owned a dog.
Ben just donned beaver caps
and attracted lovely French ladies, who earlied-to-bed
when he was early to rise. Gay Parisian moths to a flame burning
with New World life, they were. Giggling in French. Obsessed
with their own dogged desires.

OK, so the thought of it gives a little lift. But just a little.
I'm too depressed for anything drastic.

Mrs. Galway Goes to Night School

In the school parking lot, near the curb, waiting
for the last bell to ring, she sits on her torn vinyl bus
driver's seat reading *A Portrait of the Artist as a Young Man.*
Irish literature. A waste, her husband
scolds. But she insists, convinced
there is some stop she missed, some girl back there
waiting alone in black and white.

Hers is a stubborn blood. It is the island of ripped roots
somehow pressed on her palms.
It's been mapped by tavern cartographers: nights
of smoke and rain, tweed and sadness.

Her eyes are tired. Her three boys
ask where she is going Tuesday and Thursday nights.
And each dawn, as the motor idles, hunched
within its canary warmth, she reads, door pursed,
brow furrowed, until the bus before her roars off
and she feels the tug of routine, the knot
of another day.

Mrs. Galway, staring down skies from the closed
windows of her bus, morning, afternoon,
morning, great wheel reverberating under hand.
She considers truth, beauty, art
in the exhaust of red-blinking stops, sits
above the gears, breathes the grind and grumble
of her small engine.

Laughter, loudness, eternal youth
press the back of her driver's seat. Up ahead, time runs
a stop sign. And Dublin? It is always the next turn: gleaming
streets, arched church doors,
soot-stoned walls and iron bells, abbey-cold.
She'll unpurse the door, she thinks.
She'll cross and rejoice.

THE INDIFFERENT WORLD

The Death of Narcissus

October, and the glen
resounds with want,
wind, yellow rain of birch leaves.

The face and body wander,
driven by disdain,
downhill where earth
and echo
hold their breath.

From a distance, silver
eye lashed by dying buttonbush.
At its flanks,
the warmth of moss
pressing palms and knees.

Hemlock, sky, clouds
above and again in the depths
frame first the face,
then two deltoids of desire
tensing as he leans hard
over the stillness of self,
sensing a virgin desire.

Lowering his lips, he
feels the coolness of this first
kiss, never noticing the shadow
his beauty casts
over these violated waters.

Astapova Station

I think of Tolstoy, November of his life,
steel wool beard caught
on the sheepskin of his collar. He's stealing into night,
steam from the engine of his lungs
twisting gaunt and ghostly
through the air, rising, dwindling, clinging
to sky: the breaths of a lifetime.

The old writer still shows an instinct
for drama, abandoning wife, estate, every past chapter
for a train, an iron *deus ex machina*
that sways his body till dizziness forces him to the refuge
of Astapova. Here he can restore order, touch paper schedules,
see the starch of a stationmaster's uniform.
But first, he lies down—a moment
like all others, he thinks—on an oak bench burnished
smooth by passengers.

Tonight their spirits
mingle, restless, eyeing the great
clock like suspicious policemen. Tolstoy lifts his feet, hears the clunk
of his self-made shoes echo from the rafters. There's dried mud on his soles,
caked pieces of Russia falling
on guttered slats of wood. The weight of fever
begins to climb his chest. It stretches its claws to his temples,
rests on him, rapid heartbeat blanketing heartbeats
through the night.

He starts, thinks he hears Sofya's voice. Did he sleep? To board
the train! Is it still here, then? Is that it—black and abandoned,
frozen to cold tracks? Is it this—oblong, silver
car blinking in snow, readying to open its doors?

Tolstoy's mouth opens, breaking
mucus, a milky thread between the lips. His tongue is a fullness,
but he must know: arrival or departure?
The window! The red and black sign reading "Astapova"!
The stationmaster's warm hand closing his eyelids.

Dirt Shy

Adults don't know—or maybe forget—the touch
      of the ground.
The earth remembers us, though, remembers
      because it recalls
itself: iron, oxygen, silicon, bone, magnesium, tooth,
      sulfur, tendon, nickel,
muscle, calcium—on loan, payable upon receipt
      with particulate interest.
Don't begrudge the earth its cold, its dampness,
      its suffocating love;
think instead of the waiting games of youth,
      the hide and go seek.
Crouched at the house corner under the mountain
      laurel, I once answered
the earth's shyness, watched as it darkened
      my jean's knee patch.
Only the wind, the sliding clouds, the sound of leaves,
      and occasional car tires
on the sandy corner of our street—that and reticent
      earth blackening my knees,
excusing itself—the sodden chill of its upstretched
      palms of clay,
thankful for my kind understanding. Polite, it never
      broached our distant play
date, not to one so young, so busy with the wonderful
      invincibility of it all.

Jacob Wrestling

At dusk, my body carving
nothingness.

Outside, the greater nothingness—taut sky
stretched, stakes pounded in foreign ravines.

Sycamores hold the wolf moon,
pinch stars shut until I am Jonah
swallowed by leviathan air,
I am Jacob wrestling nothingness,
despair.

Doppelgängers were never
stranger, bound
by these scratchy ropes of being,
muscular arms struggling
against an intimate friction.

My head rings with the bark
of ironwood. We collapse,
crushing undergrowth.
I bleed sumac and mayflower,
smell of fern and bruised hemlock.

Entangled in weeds thickened
with the past, I am encompassed,
choked by my future's thick,
its lovely.

"Inhale the world's nothingness,"
says the hot breath pressing my ear.
"Breathe its wet, its luxuriant!"

Until I want to tap out
on the angel's oily wing. I want
to give myself over to the dark,
to the sweet release of submission.

Subterranean

My childhood home is empty but still warm,
as if my young father and mother sneaked
out at the last minute, clasping coats,
hastily grabbing secrets to their chests.

In the living room, Hotei's hands
hold the gourd of his belly tight
with hoarded luck.
On the ottoman, the glass eyes of my mother's
porcelain doll drift
to the door, a fissure mining its left cheek.

There's a mug on the kitchen table, bottom
dark with freeze-dried coffee. On the stove,
creepers of tea-kettle steam rise
from the nozzle.

The seared joker cards—those I cooked
so many years ago—peek from the toaster,
still burning with resentment. Below,
the earth cellar waits.
Root of all sleep.

Universal Truths from the Parlor

Holding the chewed bit of his pipe stem before his unshaved face,
my grandfather said, "Some words are flimsy yokes, a failure
to domesticate horned abstractions." I was silent because my

grandfather seldom spoke and we were alone in his parlor late
in the day and I thought he spoke of the devil. "You understand
this, boy?" he said, like he'd just noticed me. I nodded yes

and prayed he'd not follow up like my teachers at school
when we longed for recess. "Universe," he smiled bitterly, shaking
his head. Before us, a bolt of sun traced sash and muntin lines

against the floor. "You see this cloud of dust motes?" A toothed
pipe stem pointed at the bright slanting emptiness, the tether
of warmth harnessing carpet to window. "There's your universe."

A fading meteor of spit jumped from his lips as he blew a burst
of anemic air at it and fell into a fit of coughing. I thought he might
die. The motes realigned before settling back into their orbits.

Fire on Scribner Hill

Up on Scribner Road, some woman,
feral-haired, a floral-print dress sapped by sun
and the light of years.

She's stopping, walking, stopping,
cellphone pressed against the ache
of her ear.

Note the fierce edge of shinbones,
the black ankle socks strangled in boots so heavy
they wrinkle macadam and stir the heat waves.

She's speaking, all right, but it's a fire drill
mistaken for real. Her words fight through
the emergency exit—tumbling out of order, elbowing

each other, breaking into unruly letters,
white smoke sounding the sky
in search of higher meaning.

The Physics of Aging

I. Einstein Says

In space, aging trips against air
so thin it's unseen; the march
to mortality stumbles on star-
light, slows like satellite
parabolas raking the soft black
silt of a summer night. In this
empty silence, Einstein says,
age gets silently sucked
into vacuums of immensity,
of immortality. Time
slows. God yields.

II. Story of the Star Sailor

Time jammed on noon Eastern
Standard, the astronaut peered
through his bubble helmet, swiped
a fat, clumsy glove at some
celestial smudge that turned out
to be inside the polycarbonate.
Squinting scientifically, he verified
that Ponce de León,
Conquistador of Death, got
as far as the Pleiades in his age-
old quest. Said star
sailor felt for the reassurance
of his vent pad—carafes of cupped
oxygen from Cape Canaveral—
then sipped of time, borrowed
and decanted. No moments later,
he transmitted coordinates
to Houston: "Spanish flag
floating beside Taurus, over."
The astronaut waved
his immense hand at the blue planet
below. With youthful indiscretion,
he coined his upcoming
reentry "the second coming."

III. Dust to Dust

Here I humbly shave
before a thinner space,
the thrift of a mirror.
Its silver truths shift
in hydrogen clouds. Swirling
a bath towel, I observe
the distant whorls of me, white
stubble hidden in nebula
of steam and Barbasol. Within
seconds, unbeknownst
to mankind, the second coming
will shred Einstein's
sky, bleeding the blue
days upon us.

Mortality

It waits
outside the house,
stoic as a crouched cat
tensed in tall grass.

It bides the familiar: morning
smoke from the flue,
night windows—lozenges
of light with a head
passing by inside.

There will be no
sudden charges, no rebel
yells. It is, simply,
time: The door unlocks,
opens, coughs up
a man—another assassin
of days, years, decades.
Another body.

That done, it leaves—
indifferent, never gloating.

The house remains
dark as a curtained hearse,
cold-breathed chimney
its sole historian.

What Is Past

Nabokov said, "Speak, Memory,"
and it did. Mine, however,
is mute.
Though I might dream
it, I cannot remember
my last drink
of ale in a smoky
underground bar, the last taste
of red wine and tannin
against the cat-tongued roof
of my mouth. Even, late
in the night,
the last time I cried,
tasting salt that proved
I was alive.

Earthbound

Running in a Maine rain
beside the dirt shoulder
of Powhatan Road,
I become wet historian
recording the sodden gravities:
cloven-hoof pools from a lone
whitetail's walk
before he veered into the wood,
white McDonald's bag crumpled
softly on the entrails
of its soaked innards,
the sandy chevron
of a light pickup's
wayward tire.

What's gone is ghost,
but rhythmic feet beat on,
stubborn life that doesn't know
better, pulled stride to stride
by the shadow of inverted
reflections—a deeper, darker
runner
racing the cracked black
lightning on this rain glare
below me
and above him,
sole to sole...
mile for mile.

Samsara

After years of meditation, the Buddha found
my problem—I cling to life,
I cannot release, I am no sooner dead
than crawling back, hours or days later,
as apparent man, woman,
fire ant, tiger, pelican, newt, box turtle,
hemlock tree, narwhal, salmon, roadside
weed. Clinging to a new womb, sac, egg, seed.
Thirsty for more warmth, mothers, suns. Crying
for the feel of water, food, breath.

Again and again, the barb of my beetle leg's clinch,
the proboscis of my mosquito want, the bristle
of my moth antennae's search. I crave. I need.
I suck from the marrow of my prison. I cannot
recall the womb that recalls me.

Insomnia

Three is the loneliest number on a clock
when the night can't save you.

No doubt it is the constellated tug,
a conspiracy of stars, the silent, primal

voice that whispers the uselessness,
that grinds greater gears,

that mocks the hubris of careful plans,
set alarms. Every blanketed life around you

sleeps safe and happy and secure
like nothing can touch them, like change

has made its exception, named it you,
and passed finally over the frosted roof.

The Irony of Lost Cats

Each evening as I walk suburban streets
between dead rows of telephone
poles, I admire the gallery of plastic-sleeved posters
stapled to splintered bark. All the feline fugitives,
heads bleached by the sun, have that wan-whiskered
look of the ninth life. No one scribbles down the number
because no one recognizes them. No one but the coyotes
and the fisher cats—the lost long ago found, the reward
long since cashed in.

Grave Parable

In church school, no
innocent knew
that a bent man
collapsing under crossed
wood was gravity's
metaphor already trying
their scuffed shoes
on for size.

Dream of the Yellow Jackets

Dared by yellow jackets, I approach
the hive, lay my hand on its soft paper

thrum, clench my eyes, courting
stings of violation and venom.

Instead, I sense trooping tarsi
probing the wall's warmth—feel

the swarm, the dance, the diaphanous
orgy of wings, the black and sun-striped

belts, each echoing my palm's heat,
each tracing my lifeline's poem,

journeying from creased birth
to branching death and back,

the buzz a gentle current coursing
through my combed hollows of being

until I become the paper thrum,
the hive for wasps to build and birth in,

to occupy and leave an airy charcoal shell
as the woods about me yellow and shiver,

as the world curls cold and bare
under October's hardening sky.

Jazz Funeral for Fall

I feel most alive
in fall's chromatic death.
Stay. It is the sugar maple leaves'
sweet suffocation in red; the yellow riffs
of birch, beech, poplar; the funereal
browns of bigtooth aspens as they blow
earthward, scratch pavement,
slide-slip, catch
in clots of cold November mud.
They smell of the sun one day,
sod the next,
but alive in their way,
singing that decomposed song
of the siren dead.

At the rear of the procession,
stepping to the beat
behind the pall bearers' coda, I don't imagine
views from the other side will help.
For the dead, death
is sensuously bankrupt.

New World Order

After a few years, my fears
grow Newtonian in design.

Ink dries in my book.
The calligraphy of calculations,

once unsteady scratches
on paper, hardens to dark

loops & arches & vectors
of beauty, order, predictability.

Fact: The sun rises in the east
& I will not fly. The sun nests

in the west & I no longer climb
the ribbed esophagi of skyscrapers

to peer from observation decks.
There's a certain pride in the defeat

& submission of chaos, in knowing
a building's peristalsis will never pull

me down in blind, autonomic tugs
(need of the boa, chance of the bat).

No, not that. Not
for the cautious likes of me.

Song

Outside in the subzero sun,
ice glints on black branches.

Look, a single cardinal—
small drop of blood

high in the tree
God warned us off.

Star Sailor

Hands big as the Crab Nebula,
raw knuckles atop metacarpal
rakes, skin mottled with islands
of milk and cold clay.

Rictus grip on net, leaning hard
against nothingness, skiff riding the star
trough of Corona Borealis.

Neck caged by cords, Adam's apple
tied by swallowed knot of grunts,
the star sailor trolls heady depths
for dwarfs and giants, reds and blues,
Greek heroes and beasts
pinned like icy insects
on silky black celestial seas.

Earthmen in space-station portals mouth
hails and jeers as his ship passes:
"Net holes too large! Fabric too weak!"
But the sailor drifts on,
leaning, pulling against the grace
of infinity.

There is dignity, even in losing a comet,
pride, even in watching it flop
against the firmament's hull and leap
into the bearded current of Capricorn.

And what of meteors that get away?
You cannot harvest what will not be rescued.
A sailor toils on, sniffing open clusters,
tacking from whirlpool galaxies,
hauling in silence and loneliness
for a galley that will never feed him.

The Builder at Work

It's the first moments after she leaves
that the house feels emptiest, a gutted
gourd still damp with human voice,
laughter, touch. In her wake, a lingering
scent of Chanel, a thinning of the familiar.
I inhale. My ribs rise. I try holding air
until my chest aches with her, but she
fades to the rafters, presses through pine-
paneled knots and seams, seeks cloud
and star, leaving me hostage to myself.
I have to busy this hand and build:
grip the warm hammer's handle,
drive despair from noisy nail heads,
ignore the blueprints of pity. I am
anomaly—the builder who marks
four walls that would measure him.

Acknowledgments

The following poems, some in slightly different form, first appeared in the following magazines:

Amethyst Arsenic: "Insomnia"
Angle Journal of Poetry: "Epistolary," "The Builder at Work"
Grasslimb: "Another Country"
Gray's Sporting Journal: "Trigger"
Kentucky Review: "Jiggety-Jig," "3:30"
Muddy River Poetry Review: "Pliny Instructs," "Star Sailor"
Off the Coast: "Barnstorming the Universe," "Tonsillectomy"
Petrichor Machine: "Deer Stand," "Provide, Provide"
Silver Birch Press: "The Death of Narcissus"
Splash of Red: "A Sound Unanswered"
Wolf Moon Journal: "Thompson Lake: August 23, 2008"

Cover photo, "Water Surface," by Karolina Grabowska; author photo by Jill Craft; cover and interior book design by Diane Kistner; Chaparral Pro text and titling

About FutureCycle Press

FutureCycle Press is dedicated to publishing lasting English-language poetry books, chapbooks, and anthologies in both print-on-demand and Kindle editions. Founded in 2007 by long-time independent editor/publishers and partners Diane Kistner and Robert S. King, the press incorporated as a non-profit in 2012. A number of our editors are distinguished poets and writers in their own right, and we have been actively involved in the small press movement going back to the early seventies.

The FutureCycle Poetry Book Prize and honorarium is awarded annually for the best full-length volume of poetry we publish in a calendar year. Introduced in 2013, our Good Works projects are anthologies devoted to issues of universal significance, with all proceeds donated to a related worthy cause. Our Selected Poems series highlights contemporary poets with a substantial body of work to their credit; with this series we strive to resurrect work that has had limited distribution and is now out of print.

We are dedicated to giving all of the authors we publish the care their work deserves, making our catalog of titles the most diverse and distinguished it can be, and paying forward any earnings to fund more great books.

We've learned a few things about independent publishing over the years. We've also evolved a unique, resilient publishing model that allows us to focus mainly on vetting and preserving for posterity poetry collections of exceptional quality without becoming overwhelmed with bookkeeping and mailing, fundraising activities, or taxing editorial and production "bubbles." To find out more, come see us at www.futurecycle.org.

The FutureCycle Poetry Book Prize

All full-length volumes of poetry published by FutureCycle Press in a given calendar year are considered for the annual FutureCycle Poetry Book Prize. This allows us to consider each submission on its own merits, outside of the context of a contest. Too, the judges see the finished book, which will have benefitted from the beautiful book design and strong editorial gloss we are famous for.

The book ranked the best in judging is announced as the prize-winner in the subsequent year. There is no fixed monetary award; instead, the winning poet receives an honorarium of 20% of the total net royalties from all poetry books and chapbooks the press sold online in the year the winning book was published. The winner is also accorded the honor of being on the panel of judges for the next year's competition; all judges receive copies of all contending books to keep for their personal library.

www.ingramcontent.com/pod-product-compliance
Lightning Source LLC
Chambersburg PA
CBHW072359090426
42741CB00012B/3081